Best Kids' KNOCK-KNOCK Jokes EVER!

VOLUME 2

Highlights Press
Honesdale, Pennsylvania

Cover Design by Colleen Pidell
Contributing Illustrators: David Coulson, Kelly Kennedy, Pat N. Lewis, Neil Numberman, Rich Powell, Kevin Rechin, Rick Stromoski, Pete Whitehead, Mark Corcoran

Published by Highlights Press
815 Church Street
Honesdale, Pennsylvania 18431
ISBN: 978-1-68437-246-1
Manufactured in Mattoon, IL, USA
Mfg. 07/2022

First edition
Visit our website at Highlights.com.
10 9 8 7 6 5

CONTENTS

DOG DIGS

Knock, knock.

Who's there?

A bonus.

A bonus who?

A bonus what a dog likes to chew.

Knock, knock.

Who's there?

Beagle.

Beagle who?

Beagle with cream cheese.

Knock, knock.

Who's there?

Aware.

Aware who?

"Aware, aware has my little dog gone?"

Knock, knock.

Who's there?

Bow.

Bow who?

Not bow who, *bowwow*!

Knock, knock.

Who's there?

Terrier.

Terrier who?

I'm terrier-fied of the dark!

Knock, knock.

Who's there?

Sheena.

Sheena who?

Sheena lost dog around here?

Knock, knock.

Who's there?

Bark.

Bark who?

Bark your car in the driveway.

Knock, knock.

Who's there?

Eileen.

Eileen who?

Eileen over to pet the dog.

Knock, knock.

Who's there?

Defense.

Defense who?

Defense has a hole in it—that's how our dog got loose.

Knock, knock.

Who's there?

Irish.

Irish who?

Irish I could get a puppy!

Knock, knock.

Who's there?

Alibi.

Alibi who?

Alibi the dog a new squeaky toy.

Knock, knock.

Who's there?

Ooze.

Ooze who?

Ooze a good dog?

Knock, knock.

Who's there?

Heidi.

Heidi who?

Heidi bones in de yard.

Knock, knock.

Who's there?

Kenya.

Kenya who?

Kenya walk my dog for me?

Knock, knock.

Who's there?

Leash.

Leash who?

Leash you could do is open the door.

Knock, knock.

Who's there?

Champ.

Champ who?

Champ-oo the dog.
He needs a bath!

Knock, knock.

Who's there?

Patsy.

Patsy who?

Patsy dog on the head.
He likes it!

Knock, knock.

Who's there?

Akita.

Akita who?

I need Akita open the door.

Knock, knock.

Who's there?

Pooch.

Pooch who?

Pooch your coat on—it's cold outside.

Knock, knock.

Who's there?

Doug.

Doug who?

Doug a hole in the yard.

Knock, knock.

Who's there?

Samoa.

Samoa who?

Get Samoa food for the dog, please.

Knock, knock.

Who's there?

Paws.

Paws who?

Paws-itively delighted to see you!

Knock, knock.

Who's there?

Lab.

Lab who?

Labracadabra!

Knock, knock.

Who's there?

Bargain.

Bargain who?

Bargain up the wrong tree.

Knock, knock.

Who's there?

Harry.

Harry who?

Harry dogs go to the groomer.

Knock, knock.

Who's there?

Poodle.

Poodle who?

Poodle little mustard on my hot dog.

Knock, knock.

Who's there?

Canoe.

Canoe who?

Canoe help me give the dog a bath?

Knock, knock.

Who's there?

Collie.

Collie who?

Collie doctor. I feel sick.

Knock, knock.

Who's there?

Fido.

Fido who?

Fido known you were sick, I would have brought soup.

FUNNIES ON THE FARM

Knock, knock.

Who's there?

Candy.

Candy who?

Candy cow jump over de moon?

Knock, knock.

Who's there?

Pig.

Pig who?

Pig up your feet or you'll trip.

Knock, knock.

Who's there?

Moscow.

Moscow who?

Moscows moo, but some don't.

Knock, knock.

Who's there?

Sheep.

Sheep who?

Sheep-ers! It's just me.

Knock, knock.

Who's there?

Chicken.

Chicken who?

Better chicken the oven—
something's burning.

Knock, knock.

Who's there?

Cows.

Cows who?

Cows say "moo," not "who."

Knock, knock.

Who's there?

Farmer.

Farmer who?

I hope I get a dog farmer birthday.

Knock, knock.

Who's there?

Eliza.

Eliza who?

Eliza wake at night counting sheep.

Knock, knock.

Who's there?

Phyllis.

Phyllis who?

Phyllis trough up with water, please. The cows are thirsty!

Knock, knock.

Who's there?

Mule.

Mule who?

Mule miss me, won't you?

Knock, knock.

Who's there?

Calf.

Calf who?

I calf to tell you something.

Knock, knock.

Who's there?

Hens.

Hens who?

Hens up, we've got you surrounded!

Knock, knock.

Who's there?

Udder.

Udder who?

Would you like to hear an udder knock-knock joke?

Knock, knock.

Who's there?

Cowhide.

Cowhide who?

Cowhide if she sees you coming.

Knock, knock.

Who's there?

Wool.

Wool who?

Wool you go to the movies with me?

Knock, knock.

Who's there?

Chicken ladies.

Chicken ladies who?

A chicken ladies eggs.

Knock, knock.

Who's there?

Moo.

Moo who?

Make up your mind! Are you a cow or an owl?

Knock, knock.

Who's there?

Pigment.

Pigment who?

Pigment a lot to me, but he ran away.

Knock, knock.

Who's there?

Goat.

Goat who?

Goat to the door and find out!

Knock, knock.

Who's there?

Weed.

Weed who?

Weed better go and milk the cows.

Knock, knock.

Who's there?

Genoa.

Genoa who?

Genoa how to milk a cow?

Knock, knock.

Who's there?

Cock-a-doodle.

Cock-a-doodle who?

Not cock-a-doodle who, you silly chicken, *cock-a-doodle-doo*!

Knock, knock.

Who's there?

Dairy.

Dairy who?

Dairy goes! Let's catch him!

Knock, knock.

Who's there?

Gretel.

Gretel who?

Gretel long, little doggie.

Knock, knock.

Who's there?

Chesterfield.

Chesterfield who?

Chesterfield full of cows.

Knock, knock.

Who's there?

Farmer.

Farmer who?

Farmer people here than there were last year.

Knock, knock.

Who's there?

Udder.

Udder who?

Udder people let me in. Why won't you?

Knock, knock.

Who's there?

Heifer.

Heifer who?

Heifer dollar is better than none.

Knock, knock.

Who's there?

Fleece.

Fleece who?

Fleece Navidad.

Knock, knock.

Who's there?

Dairy.

Dairy who?

Dairy Christmas.

Knock, knock.

Who's there?

Moo.

Moo who?

Happy Moo Year!

Knock, knock.

Who's there?

Cow.

Cow who?

Cow much longer are you going to put up with all this knocking?

Knock, knock.

Who's there?

Chick.

Chick who?

Chick out my new skateboard!

Knock, knock.

Who's there?

Ewe.

Ewe who?

Ewe are my best friend.

Knock, knock.

Who's there?

Cymbals.

Cymbals who?

Cymbals have horns and others don't.

Knock, knock.

Who's there?

Barbara.

Barbara who?

"Barbara black sheep, have you any wool?"

Knock, knock.

Who's there?

Interrupting cow.

Interrup—

MOOOOO!

SAFARI SO GOOD

Knock, knock.

Who's there?

Rhino.

Rhino who?

Rhino every knock-knock joke there is.

Knock, knock.

Who's there?

Giraffe.

Giraffe who?

Giraffe anything to eat? I'm hungry!

Knock, knock.

Who's there?

Lion.

Lion who?

You're lion down on the job again.

Knock, knock.

Who's there?

Hyena.

Hyena who?

Hyena tree sits the beautiful bald eagle.

Knock, knock.

Who's there?

Meerkat.

Meerkat who?

Meerkat, 'meer kitty, come get your treat!

Knock, knock.

Who's there?

An elephant.

An elephant who?

An elephant who is lost.

Knock, knock.

Who's there?

Hip.

Hip who?

Hippopotamus!

Knock, knock.

Who's there?

Safari.

Safari who?

Safari so good!

Knock, knock.

Who's there?

Fiona.

Fiona who?

Fiona lookout for a lion.

Knock, knock.

Who's there?

Sherwood.

Sherwood who?

Sherwood like to see a zebra.

Knock, knock.

Who's there?

Tusk.

Tusk who?

Tusk, tusk, it looks like rain.

Knock, knock.

Who's there?

Aardvark.

Aardvark who?

Aardvark a hundred miles to see you.

Knock, knock.

Who's there?

Gnu.

Gnu who?

Gnu you'd ask me that.

Knock, knock.

Who's there?

Adeline.

Adeline who?

You should Adeline to your drawing of an elephant.

Knock, knock.

Who's there?

Lion.

Lion who?

Lion on your doorstep. Open up!

Knock, knock.

Who's there?

Wildebeest.

Wildebeest who?

Wildebeest turn back into a prince?

Knock, knock.

Who's there?

Giraffe.

Giraffe who?

Sorry I'm late. I was stuck in a giraffe-ic jam.

Knock, knock.

Who's there?

Savannah.

Savannah who?

She's Savannah great time!

Knock, knock.

Who's there?

Lionel.

Lionel who?

Lionel bite you if you put your head in its mouth.

Knock, knock.

Who's there?

Hippo.

Hippo who?

Hippo birthday to you!

BIRD BONANZA

Knock, knock.

Who's there?

Toucan.

Toucan who?

Toucan play this game.

Knock, knock.

Who's there?

Ostrich.

Ostrich who?

Ostrich my arms up to the sky.

Knock, knock.

Who's there?

Why do owls go.

Why do owls go who?

Because that's how they talk, silly!

Knock, knock.

Who's there?

Deduct.

Deduct who?

Deduct went, "Quack, quack."

Knock, knock.

Who's there?

Kiwi.

Kiwi who?

Kiwi go out to play?

Knock, knock.

Who's there?

Crows.

Crows who?

Crows the door. It's cold outside!

Knock, knock.

Who's there?

Wren.

Wren who?

Wren you're finished, please put it away.

Knock, knock.

Who's there?

Cook.

Cook who?

Hey, who are you calling a cuckoo?

Knock, knock.

Who's there?

Who.

Who who?

I didn't know you spoke Owl!

Knock, knock.

Who's there?

Stork.

Stork who?

Better stork up on food before the storm.

Knock, knock.

Who's there?

Ernest.

Ernest who?

Ernest is full of eggs!

Knock, knock.

Who's there?

Macaw.

Macaw who?

Macaw has a flat tire—can you help?

Knock, knock.

Who's there?

Turkey.

Turkey who?

Turkey, open door.

Knock, knock.

Who's there?

Allison.

Allison who?

Allison to the birds sing every morning.

Knock, knock.

Who's there?

Beak.

Beak who?

Beak careful with that!

Knock, knock.

Who's there?

Dove.

Dove who?

I'd dove to stay, but I have to go!

Knock, knock.

Who's there?

Earl E.

Earl E. who?

Earl E. bird gets the worm.

Knock, knock.

Who's there?

Owls.

Owls who?

Of course they do—everybody knows that.

Knock, knock.

Who's there?

Ibis.

Ibis who?

Ibis just leaving.

Knock, knock.

Who's there?

Quack.

Quack who?

You quack me up with all these knock-knock jokes.

Knock, knock.

Who's there?

Hawk.

Hawk who?

Well this is hawk-ward.

Knock, knock.

Who's there?

Sparrow.

Sparrow who?

Sparrow me the details and let me in.

Knock, knock.

Who's there?

Talon.

Talon who?

Talon everyone I know.

Knock, knock.

Who's there?

Alberts.

Alberts who?

Do Alberts fly south for the winter?

Knock, knock.

Who's there?

Wing.

Wing. who?

Wing, wing, wing. Hello?

Knock, knock.

Who's there?

Heron.

Heron who?

Heron the floor of the salon.

Knock, knock.

Who's there?

Goose.

Goose who?

No, you goose who!

Knock, knock.

Who's there?

Tweet.

Tweet who?

Tweet me nicely, and I'll tweet you nicely too.

Knock, knock.

Who's there?

Hannah.

Hannah who?

"Hannah partridge in a pear tree."

Knock, knock.

Who's there?

Owl.

Owl who?

Owl aboard!

Knock, knock.

Who's there?

A parrot.

A parrot who?

A-parrot-ly I'm at the wrong door.

Knock, knock.

Who's there?

Caw.

Caw who?

Stop in the name of the caw!

Knock, knock.

Who's there?

Robin.

Robin who?

Robin banks is wrong.

Knock, knock.

Who's there?

Swan.

Swan who?

Just swan to say hi.

Knock, knock.

Who's there?

Thrush.

Thrush who?

We have plenty of time. What's thrush?

Knock, knock.

Who's there?

Baby owl.

Baby owl who?

Baby owl see you later or baby owl just call you.

Knock, knock.

Who's there?

Aviary.

Aviary who?

Aviary Merry Christmas to you!

Knock, knock.

Who's there?

Raven.

Raven who?

I've been raven about you to all my friends!

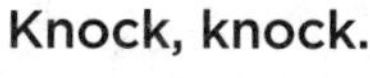

Knock, knock.

Who's there?

Fannie.

Fannie who?

Fannie body asks, I've gone birdwatching.

CREEPY CRAWLY CRACKUPS

Knock, knock.

Who's there?

Spider.

Spider who?

In spider everything, I still like you.

Knock, knock.

Who's there?

Abby.

Abby who?

Abby stung me on the nose!

Knock, knock.

Who's there?

Termites.

Termites who?

Termite's the night we're going out.

Knock, knock.

Who's there?

Earwig.

Earwig who?

Earwig go again.

Knock, knock.

Who's there?

Beehive.

Beehive who?

Beehive yourself or else.

Knock, knock.

Who's there?

Thumping.

Thumping who?

Thumping green and thlimy is crawling up your leg.

Knock, knock.

Who's there?

Worm.

Worm who?

Worm my keys go?

Knock, knock.

Who's there?

Gnats.

Gnats who?

Gnats not a bit funny.

Knock, knock.

Who's there?

Bee.

Bee who?

Bee-cause I like you, I came to visit.

Knock, knock.

Who's there?

Theresa.

Theresa who?

Theresa fly in my soup!

Knock, knock.

Who's there?

Flea.

Flea who?

Flea blind mice.

Knock, knock.

Who's there?

Army ants.

Army ants who?

Army ants coming for tea?

Knock, knock.

Who's there?

Roach.

Roach who?

Roach you a letter. Did you get it?

Knock, knock.

Who's there?

Moth.

Moth who?

I moth tell you that I like you!

Knock, knock.

Who's there?

Bezoar.

Bezoar who?

Bezoar black and yellow.

Knock, knock.

Who's there?

Weevil.

Weevil who?

Weevil stay only a few minutes.

Knock, knock.

Who's there?

Cass.

Cass who?

Cass more flies with honey than vinegar.

Knock, knock.

Who's there?

Zombies.

Zombies who?

Zombies make honey, and zombies don't.

Knock, knock.

Who's there?

Amos.

Amos who?

A mosquito.

Knock, knock.

Who's there?

An udder.

An udder who?

An udder mosquito.

Knock, knock.

Who's there?

Yeti.

Yeti who?

Yeti 'nother mosquito.

Knock, knock.

Who's there?

Stew.

Stew who?

Stew many mosquitoes out here. Let's go inside.

Knock, knock.

Who's there?

Henrietta.

Henrietta who?

Henrietta bug and now he's sick.

Knock, knock.

Who's there?

Bug spray.

Bug spray who?

Bug spray that snakes and birds will stay away.

Knock, knock.

Who's there?

Wasp.

Wasp who?

I wasp planning to tell you . . .

Knock, knock.

Who's there?

Wood ant.

Wood ant who?

Don't be afraid. I wood ant hurt a fly!

Knock, knock.

Who's there?

Don.

Don who?

Don scream, but there's a spider by your foot.

Knock, knock.

Who's there?

Arctics.

Arctics who?

Arctics going to bite me in the woods?

Knock, knock.

Who's there?

Usher.

Usher who?

Usher do love butterflies.

Knock, knock.

Who's there?

Honeycomb.

Honeycomb who?

**Honeycomb your hair—
it's tangled.**

Knock, knock.

Who's there?

Fleas.

Fleas who?

**"Fleas a jolly good
fellow . . ."**

Knock, knock.

Who's there?

Mantis.

Mantis who?

Mantis sandwich tastes great!

Knock, knock.

Who's there?

Beetle.

Beetle who?

Beetle little more flour into the dough, will you?

Knock, knock.

Who's there?

Indonesia.

Indonesia who?

Spiders make me weak Indonesia.

Knock, knock.

Who's there?

Chimney.

Chimney who?

Chimney Cricket. Have you seen Pinocchio?

Knock, knock.

Who's there?

Worm.

Worm who?

Worm in here, isn't it?

Knock, knock.

Who's there?

Ant hill.

Ant hill who?

Ant hill we meet again.

Knock, knock.

Who's there?

Waffle.

Waffle who?

Waffle lot of fireflies out tonight.

Knock, knock.

Who's there?

Honeybee.

Honeybee who?

Honeybee a dear and get me some juice.

Knock, knock.

Who's there?

Grub.

Grub who?

Grub hold of my hand and let's get out of here.

HORSE HUMOR

Knock, knock.

Who's there?

Yukon.

Yukon who?

Yukon lead a horse to water, but you can't make it drink.

Knock, knock.

Who's there?

Mustang.

Mustang who?

I mustang this lovely picture on the wall.

Knock, knock.

Who's there?

Pasture.

Pasture who?

Pasture bedtime, isn't it?

Knock, knock.

Who's there?

Annapolis.

Annapolis who?

Annapolis a good treat to give a horse.

Knock, knock.

Who's there?

Mane.

Mane who?

Mane to tell you I was stopping by.

Knock, knock.

Who's there?

Trot.

Trot who?

Trot you would like some company.

Knock, knock.

Who's there?

Foal.

Foal who?

Foal the last time, let me in!

Knock, knock.

Who's there?

Whinny.

Whinny who?

Whinny gets home, you can ask him.

Knock, knock.

Who's there?

Saddle.

Saddle who?

Saddle be the day.

Knock, knock.

Who's there?

Stirrup.

Stirrup who?

Stirrup some hot chocolate for me, please.

Knock, knock.

Who's there?

Appaloosa.

Appaloosa who?

Appaloosa thread on my shirt.

Knock, knock.

Who's there?

Wanda.

Wanda who?

Wanda go horseback riding with me?

Knock, knock.

Who's there?

Neigh.

Neigh who?

Neigh-body listens to me!

Knock, knock.

Who's there?

Hoof.

Hoof who?

Hoof to use the bathroom. Please let me in!

Knock, knock.

Who's there?

Yee.

Yee who?

What are you? A cowboy?

CAT LAUGHS

Knock, knock.

Who's there?

Neil.

Neil who?

Neil down and pet the cat before he scratches you!

Knock, knock.

Who's there?

Me.

Me who?

You sure have a funny-sounding cat.

Knock, knock.

Who's there?

Feline.

Feline who?

I'm feline fine, thanks.

Knock, knock.

Who's there?

Cattle.

Cattle who?

Cattle purr when you pet her.

Knock, knock.

Who's there?

Kitten.

Kitten who?

I'm just kitten with you!

Knock, knock.

Who's there?

Landon.

Landon who?

Landon their feet is what cats do.

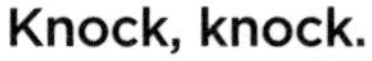

Knock, knock.

Who's there?

Meow.

Meow who?

Take meow to the ball game!

Knock, knock.

Who's there?

Zany.

Zany who?

Zany body seen the cat?

Knock, knock.

Who's there?

Howdy.

Howdy who?

Howdy cat get outside?

Knock, knock.

Who's there?

Catsup.

Catsup who?

Catsup in the tree. Want me to go get him?

Knock, knock.

Who's there?

Detail.

Detail who?

Detail of de cat is on de end.

Knock, knock.

Who's there?

Fission.

Fission who?

Fission a bowl are safe from the cat.

Knock, knock.

Who's there?

Arthur.

Arthur who?

Arthur any cats in your house?

Knock, knock.

Who's there?

Purring.

Purring who?

Purring some lemonade. Do you want some?

Knock, knock.

Who's there?

Cadillac.

Cadillac who?

Cadillac to be pet on the head.

Knock, knock.

Who's there?

Colin.

Colin who?

Colin the vet—the cat is sick!

Knock, knock.

Who's there?

Mew.

Mew who?

Let's go to the mew-seum today.

Knock, knock.

Who's there?

Cheese.

Cheese who?

Cheese a very soft cat.

Knock, knock.

Who's there?

Claws.

Claws who?

Claws the window—it's cold in here!

Knock, knock.

Who's there?

Summertime.

Summertime who?

Summertime the cat lets you pet him, and summertime he doesn't.

Knock, knock.

Who's there?

Fur.

Fur who?

Waiting fur you to open the door.

Knock, knock.

Who's there?

Isabelle.

Isabelle who?

Isabelle on the cat's collar?

Knock, knock.

Who's there?

Sophie.

Sophie who?

The cat is meowing—Sophie her.

Knock, knock.

Who's there?

Cat.

Cat who?

Cat you just let me in?

INTO THE WOODS

Knock, knock.

Who's there?

Aurora.

Aurora who?

Aurora's just come from that bear.

Knock, knock.

Who's there?

Moose.

Moose who?

Moose you be so nosy?

Knock, knock.

Who's there?

Bat.

Bat who?

Bat you can't guess.

Knock, knock.

Who's there?

Mice.

Mice who?

Mice to meet you.

Knock, knock.

Who's there?

Bunny.

Bunny who?

Bunny thing is, I've forgotten!

Knock, knock.

Who's there?

Grrr.

Grrr who?

Are you a bear or an owl?

Knock, knock.

Who's there?

Woodchuck.

Woodchuck who?

Woodchuck come to our party if we invited him?

Knock, knock.

Who's there?

Possum.

Possum who?

Possum food, please. I'm hungry!

Knock, knock.

Who's there?

Beaver E.

Beaver E. who?

Beaver E. quiet and nobody will hear us.

Knock, knock.

Who's there?

Hugh.

Hugh who?

Hugh's afraid of the big, bad wolf?

Knock, knock.

Who's there?

Moose.

Moose who?

Moose-quito bit me.

Knock, knock.

Who's there?

Andy.

Andy who?

Andy bit me again!

Knock, knock.

Who's there?

Rattle.

Rattle who?

Rattle eat that cheese if we forget to put it away.

Knock, knock.

Who's there?

Odor.

Odor who?

Odor skunks are wiser than younger skunks.

Knock, knock.

Who's there?

Bear.

Bear who?

Bear with me—I'll tell you a better joke.

Knock, knock.

Who's there?

Weasel.

Weasel who?

Weasel while you work.

Knock, knock.

Who's there?

Caribou.

Caribou who?

I caribou-t you a lot!

Knock, knock.

Who's there?

Rabbit.

Rabbit who?

**Please rabbit up for me—
it's a present for my mom.**

Knock, knock.

Who's there?

Deer.

Deer who?

Deer to be different!

Knock, knock.

Who's there?

Athena.

Athena who?

Athena mouse run past your door!

Knock, knock.

Who's there?

Gopher.

Gopher who?

Gopher help. I'm stuck in the mud!

Knock, knock.

Who's there?

Hare.

Hare who?

Hare you are!

Knock, knock.

Who's there?

Wolf pack.

Wolf pack who?

Wolf pack some food and go on a picnic.

Knock, knock.

Who's there?

Howl.

Howl who?

Howl you know unless you open the door?

Knock, knock.

Who's there?

Badger.

Badger who?

I hate to badger you, but can you let me in?

Knock, knock.

Who's there?

Esther.

Esther who?

Esther Bunny.

Knock, knock.

Who's there?

Anna.

Anna who?

Anna 'nother Esther Bunny.

Knock, knock.

Who's there?

Stella.

Stella who?

Stella 'nother Esther Bunny.

Knock, knock.

Who's there?

Harmony.

Harmony who?

Harmony more Esther Bunnies are there?!

Knock, knock.

Who's there?

Isaac.

Isaac who?

Isaac of all these Esther Bunnies!

MONKEY MANIA

Knock, knock.

Who's there?

Gorilla.

Gorilla who?

Gorilla burger for me, if you please.

Knock, knock.

Who's there?

Chimp.

Chimp who?

Chimp off the old block.

Knock, knock.

Who's there?

Monkey.

Monkey who?

Monkey won't fit. That's why I knocked!

Knock, knock.

Who's there?

Gibbon.

Gibbon who?

Gibbon my dog a bath.

Knock, knock.

Who's there?

Ape.

Ape who?

Ape, B, C, D . . .

Knock, knock.

Who's there?

Indy.

Indy who?

Indy rainforest lived di monkey.

Knock, knock.

Who's there?

Chimp.

Chimp who?

I think you mean to say, "shampoo."

Knock, knock.

Who's there?

Banana.

Banana who?

Knock, knock.

Who's there?

Banana.

Banana who?

Knock, knock.

Who's there?

Banana.

Banana who?

Knock, knock.

Who's there?

Amon.

Amon who?

Amon-key to eat all of these bananas!

Knock, knock.

Who's there?

Ivory.

Ivory who?

Ivory strong, like Tarzan!

Knock, knock.

Who's there?

Wallaby.

Wallaby who?

Wallaby a monkey's uncle!

Knock, knock.

Who's there?

Jim.

Jim who?

Jim-panzee.

Knock, knock.

Who's there?

Dare.

Dare who?

Dare is a howler monkey up in that tree.

Knock, knock.

Who's there?

Ease.

Ease who?

Ease up there, on that branch.

Knock, knock.

Who's there?

Maddie.

Maddie who?

Maddie-gascar is where lemurs live.

HISSES AND HOPS

Knock, knock.

Who's there?

Iguana.

Iguana who?

Iguana hold your hand.

Knock, knock.

Who's there?

Toad.

Toad who?

Knock-knock jokes are toad-ally awesome!

Knock, knock.

Who's there?

Gecko.

Gecko who?

Gecko-ing or you'll be late for school!

Knock, knock.

Who's there?

Alli.

Alli who?

Alligator, that's who.

Knock, knock.

Who's there?

Viper.

Viper who?

Please viper runny nose.

Knock, knock.

Who's there?

Frog.

Frog who?

Frog-ot to tell you good-bye!

Knock, knock.

Who's there?

Turtle.

Turtle who?

Got to go. Turtle-oo!

Knock, knock.

Who's there?

Toad.

Toad who?

Toad you I knew a good knock-knock joke.

Knock, knock.

Who's there?

Hisses.

Hisses who?

Hisses the last straw!

Knock, knock.

Who's there?

Dragon.

Dragon who?

You're dragon your feet again.

Knock, knock.

Who's there?

Alligator.

Alligator who?

Alligator for her birthday was a card.

Knock, knock.

Who's there?

Krista.

Krista who?

Krista frog and he'll turn into a prince!

Knock, knock.

Who's there?

Anna.

Anna who?

Anna-conda.

Knock, knock.

Who's there?

Odette.

Odette who?

Odette's a big snake!

Knock, knock.

Who's there?

Tortoise.

Tortoise who?

Tortoise all I have to say.

Knock, knock.

Who's there?

Croak.

Croak who?

Croak-et is my favorite game to play.

Knock, knock.

Who's there?

Irma.

Irma who?

Irma gonna go and catch a frog.

Knock, knock.

Who's there?

Newt.

Newt who?

What's newt with you?

Knock, knock.

Who's there?

Thea.

Thea who?

Thea later, alligator!

DINO-ROARS

Knock, knock.

Who's there?

T. rex.

T. rex who?

There's a T. rex at your door and you want to know its name?!

Knock, knock.

Who's there?

Saw.

Saw who?

Dino-saw!

Knock, knock.

Who's there?

Raptor.

Raptor who?

Raptor present for you. Happy birthday!

Knock, knock.

Who's there?

Dinosaur.

Dinosaur who?

Dinosaurs don't go who. They go *ROAR*!

Knock, knock.

Who's there?

Viola.

Viola who?

Viola dinosaurs disappear?

Knock, knock.

Who's there?

Imogen.

Imogen who?

Imogen how big a brachiosaurus was!

Knock, knock.

Who's there?

Herbivore.

Herbivore who?

Who's that girl? I never saw herbivore!

Knock, knock.

Who's there?

Thumb.

Thumb who?

Thumb dinosaurs had feathers and thumb did not.

Knock, knock.

Who's there?

Carnivore.

Carnivore who?

Carnivore drives when I want it to.

Knock, knock.

Who's there?

Fossil.

Fossil who?

Fossil last time, open the door!

Knock, knock.

Who's there?

Alec.

Alec who?

Alec to pretend I'm a pterodactyl.

Knock, knock.

Who's there?

Juneau.

Juneau who?

Did Juneau that dinosaurs existed 65 million years ago?

Knock, knock.

Who's there?

Ankylosaur.

Ankylosaur who?

Can you get me some ice? My ankylosaur.

Knock, knock.

Who's there?

Dino.

Dino who?

Dino the answer!

Knock, knock.

Who's there?

Vivaldi.

Vivaldi who?

Vivaldi dinosaur species, how can I pick a favorite?

FISH AND FRIENDS

Knock, knock.

Who's there?

Halibut.

Halibut who?

Halibut we go to the movies tonight?

Knock, knock.

Who's there?

Bass.

Bass who?

Bass the salt and pepper, please!

Knock, knock.

Who's there?

Caesar.

Caesar who?

Caesar where you find all the fish.

Knock, knock.

Who's there?

Cod.

Cod who?

Cod you red-handed with all my gummy worms!

Knock, knock.

Who's there?

Michelle.

Michelle who?

Michelle has a hermit crab inside.

Knock, knock.

Who's there?

Walrus.

Walrus who?

Why do you walrus ask that silly question?

Knock, knock.

Who's there?

Reef.

Reef who?

Reef you don't mind, can you let me in?

Knock, knock.

Who's there?

Whale.

Whale who?

Whale, whale, whale. I see your door is locked again.

Knock, knock.

Who's there?

Gwen.

Gwen who?

Gwen fishin'.

Knock, knock.

Who's there?

Porpoise.

Porpoise who?

I stopped by on porpoise to see you.

Knock, knock.

Who's there?

Shell.

Shell who?

Shell we dance?

Knock, knock.

Who's there?

Clarinet.

Clarinet who?

Clarinet-ted a fish, and now she's throwing it back!

Knock, knock.

Who's there?

Seaweed.

Seaweed who?

Seaweed come in, if only you'd open the door.

Knock, knock.

Who's there?

Minnow.

Minnow who?

Let minnow if you want to hang out.

Knock, knock.

Who's there?

Cotton.

Cotton who?

I have a fish cotton the line!

Knock, knock.

Who's there?

Crab.

Crab who?

Let's crab a bite to eat.

Knock, knock.

Who's there?

Shore.

Shore who?

Shore would like to come in.

Knock, knock.

Who's there?

Frida.

Frida who?

Frida fish their food, please!

Knock, knock.

Who's there?

Seal.

Seal who?

Seal little dog anywhere?

Knock, knock.

Who's there?

Jaws.

Jaws who?

Jaws stopped by to see if you want to go swimming.

Knock, knock.

Who's there?

Urchin.

Urchin who?

Urchin has a dimple.

Knock, knock.

Who's there?

Rhoda.

Rhoda who?

"Row, row, Rhoda boat, gently down the stream."

Knock, knock.

Who's there?

Pike.

Pike who?

Pike a card, any card.

Knock, knock.

Who's there?

Eel.

Eel who?

Eel be back.

Knock, knock.

Who's there?

Tuna.

Tuna who?

Tuna piano, and it'll sound better.

Knock, knock.

Who's there?

Mackerel.

Mackerel who?

You mackerel good sandwich.

Knock, knock.

Who's there?

Flounder.

Flounder who?

Flounder keys. Here you go!

Knock, knock.

Who's there?

Bayou.

Bayou who?

I'll bayou a treat.

Knock, knock.

Who's there?

Roxanne.

Roxanne who?

Roxanne coral make the aquarium look nice.

Knock, knock.

Who's there?

Manatee.

Manatee who?

Manatee you made needs more lemon and sugar.

Knock, knock.

Who's there?

Fin.

Fin who?

Fin-tastic to see you!

Knock, knock.

Who's there?

Tide.

Tide who?

Are you tide of knock-knock jokes yet?

Knock, knock.

Who's there?

Aspen.

Aspen who?

Aspen all day trying to catch a fish.

Knock, knock.

Who's there?

Trout.

Trout who?

Trout and about.

Knock, knock.

Who's there?

Jaws.

Jaws who?

Jaws truly!

Knock, knock.

Who's there?

Sandal.

Sandal who?

Sandal get stuck to your legs if you get them wet.

Knock, knock.

Who's there?

Herring.

Herring who?

Herring some great jokes today!

HILARIOUS HODGEPODGE

Knock, knock.

Who's there?

Kanga.

Kanga who?

Kangaroo, silly!

Knock, knock.

Who's there?

Alpaca.

Alpaca who?

Alpaca the trunk, you pack-a the suitcase.

Knock, knock.

Who's there?

Izzy.

Izzy who?

Izzy hamster in his cage?

Knock, knock.

Who's there?

Census.

Census who?

Census Saturday, let's go to the zoo.

Knock, knock.

Who's there?

Koala.

Koala who?

These are some koala-ty knock-knock jokes!

Knock, knock.

Who's there?

Icy.

Icy who?

Icy a big polar bear.

Knock, knock.

Who's there?

Juicy.

Juicy who?

Juicy the big polar bear?

Knock, knock.

Who's there?

Whom.

Whom who?

"Whom, whom on the range, where the deer and the antelope play . . ."

Knock, knock.

Who's there?

Camel.

Camel who?

Camel little closer—I have something to tell you.

Knock, knock.

Who's there?

Mammoth.

Mammoth who?

Mammoth is sthuck 'cause I'th been eatin' peanut buther.

Knock, knock.

Who's there?

Llama.

Llama who?

"Llama Yankee Doodle Dandy."

Knock, knock.

Who's there?

Bison.

Bison who?

Bison new shoes. Those are worn out!

Knock, knock.

Who's there?

Otter.

Otter who?

You otter open the door and let me in.

Knock, knock.

Who's there?

Panther.

Panther who?

Panther what I wear on my legth.

Knock, knock.

Who's there?

Tooth.

Tooth who?

Tooth or dare?

Knock, knock.

Who's there?

Rhoda.

Rhoda who?

Rhoda camel through the desert.

Knock, knock.

Who's there?

Sahara.

Sahara who?

Sahara you feeling today?

Knock, knock.

Who's there?

Zookeeper.

Zookeeper who?

Zookeeper away from me. She's mean!

Knock, knock.

Who's there?

Armadillo.

Armadillo who?

Armadillo the cards after you cut the deck.

Knock, knock.

Who's there?

Ox.

Ox who?

Ox me nicely and I'll take you out for ice cream.

Knock, knock.

Who's there?

Tail.

Tail who?

Tail me you love me!

Knock, knock.

Who's there?

Ocelot.

Ocelot who?

You ocelot of questions, don't you?

Knock, knock.

Who's there?

Yak.

Yak who?

Yak-tually, I was just leaving.

Knock, knock.

Who's there?

A herd.

A herd who?

A herd you were home, so I came over.

Knock, knock.

Who's there?

Jungle.

Jungle who?

"Jungle bells, jungle bells, jungle all the way."

Knock, knock.

Who's there?

Rich.

Rich who?

Rich animal is your favorite?

Knock, knock.

Who's there?

Furry.

Furry who?

Furry funny jokes we're telling today.

Knock, knock.

Who's there?

Zoo.

Zoo who?

Zoo should come again!